The Marketing Plan Template

By Mitta Xinindlu

Using This Book

Follow this book as if you were already using a template to write your marketing plan. Follow the guiding tips and manage your time.

About the template

One of the most important, yet often overlooked areas for the small business owner is the development of a marketing plan. An effective marketing plan will act as a reference document to help you to execute your marketing strategy. It will also help you to develop a methodical approach to creating services and products that satisfy your customers' needs.

When writing a marketing plan you need to be clear about your marketing objectives and how you're going to achieve them. A good marketing plan sets realistic and measurable objectives; includes budgets and action plans and allocates responsibilities.

Elements of a Marketing Plan

- A summary of your marketing plan
- Background analysis of your business and market
- Marketing objectives and strategy of your business
- Your marketing-mix
- Action plans and budgets
- Organisational implications and contingencies
- Evaluation and monitoring strategies
- Supporting documentation

Plan, Check, Act and Repeat

Keep it up to date

Planning your marketing should be an ongoing business activity. As the market conditions and your business change, you will need to revisit many of the ideas and strategies outlined in your marketing plan. By referring to your plan regularly, you will ensure that your business keeps heading in the right direction.

How to use the template in this book

Prior to completing the marketing plan template, consider the following:

1. **Gather together your key business documents.** This includes business plans, budgets, resumes, forecasts and registration documents. Having the right information on hand will mean you can be more accurate in your forecasts and analysis as you move through the marketing plan template.

2. **Take your time and consider your specific needs.** Work through the template at your own pace. Start by deciding which sections are relevant for your business and set aside the sections that don't apply. You can always go back to the other sections later.

3. **Decide on your audience.** It's also important to consider your audience when writing your marketing plan. Will the plan be used internally? Or will you be sharing it with

others? Deciding on the purpose of the plan can help you target your answers appropriately.

4. **Ask for some assistance.** If you aren't confident in completing the marketing plan template yourself, you can enlist the help of a professional (i.e. Business adviser or accountant) to look through your plan and provide you with advice.

To complete the template:

1. Guidance text appears throughout the document, marked by the word Guidance. Where you see a guidance note, read and then delete it. Guidance has been added to help you complete the template and should not appear in your final version.

2. Using Word's Replace function, search for {Business Name} and replace with your company name.

   a. In Word's Home ribbon, open the Find and Replace tool, choose Replace to open the Find and Replace tool. The Find and Replace dialog opens with the Replace tab selected.

   b. Enter {Business Name} in the Find what field.

   c. Enter your company name in the Replace with field.

d. Click Replace All

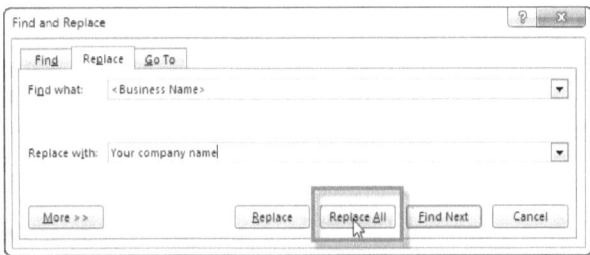

3. Replace {items in curly brackets} with your own wording.

4. Once you have finished work on the template, delete this and the following page.

5. Lastly refresh the page numbers in the table of contents.

   a. Right-mouse-click on the table of contents

   b. In the small menu that appears, choose 'Update Field' then 'Update page numbers only'.

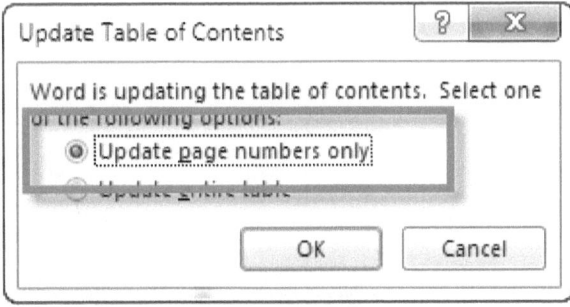

The Marketing Plan

The content of your plan should have the following topics

- Marketing plan
- Marketing plan summary

- Your business
- Business name:
- Business structure:
- Abn:
- Acn:
- Business location:
- Date established:
- Business owner(s):
- Owner/s experience
- Products or services:

- Market overview
- Target market:
- Customer profile:
- Competitor profile:

- Marketing objectives
- Goals/objectives:
- Marketing strategy
- Your strategy and marketing mix:

- Action steps
- Top 10 action steps

- Background analysis
- Business overview
- Business name
- Business structure
- Abn
- Account

- Business location
- Date established
- Business owner(s)
- Owner/s experience
- Vision statement
- Mission statement
- Business objectives
- Short term goals
- Long term goals
- Products
- Financial analysis

- Swot analysis
- Swot activity sheet

- The market overview
- Your market
- Market research and environmental/industry analysis

- Your customers
- Target customers
- Customer profile

- Your competitors
- Competitor analysis
- Competitor profile
- Your marketing

- Marketing strategy:
- Your product or service
- The pricing of your product or service
- Your position (place) in the marketplace
- Sales and distribution channels
- The promotion of your product or service

- The people in your business (salespeople, staff etc.)
- The process represents the buying experience
- The physical environment where the good/services are presented

- Productivity is an essential part of meeting a customer's needs
- Marketing activity
- Your finances
- Marketing budget {year
- Organisational implications
- Contingencies
- Monitoring/measurement activities
- Supporting documentation

Marketing Plan Summary

Guidance: Complete this page last. The marketing plan summary is a snapshot of your more detailed answers from your marketing plan. It should be easy to read and simple to follow.

Start writing here.

Your Business

Business name:

Guidance: What's your business registered business name? If you haven't registered a business name, add your proposed business name here.

Start writing here.

Business structure:

Guidance: What's the formal structure of your business? Are you a sole trader, in a partnership, a trust or company?

Start writing here.

ABN:

Guidance: What's your registered Australian Business Number?

Start writing here.

ACN:

Guidance: What's your registered Australian Company Number, if applicable?

Start writing here.

Business location:

Guidance: Where does your business operate from?

Start writing here.

Date established:

Guidance: When did you begin trading?

Start writing here.

Business owner(s):

Guidance: Who are the owners of the business?

Start writing here.

Owner/s experience:

Guidance: Create a summary of your (and other owner's) experience in the industry and any major achievements/awards.

Start writing here.

Products or Services:

Guidance: What products and/or services do you sell?

Start writing here.

Market Overview

Target market:

Guidance: In one or two sentences, summarise the key statistics for your target market. This may include the size and growth potential of your market, as well as key demographics such as age, gender, income level etc.

Start writing here.

Customer profile:

Guidance: What's the profile of an ideal customer for your business? In one or two sentences, clearly define your ideal customer - their needs, buying patterns and motivations for buying.

Start writing here.

Competitor profile:

Guidance: What's the profile of a typical competitor for your business? What marketing mix do they use? Have you identified any gaps in their marketing strategy?}

Start writing here.

Marketing Objectives

Goals/objectives:

Guidance: In one or two sentences, summarise the key marketing objectives for your business. Your objectives may be financial, with a goal to increase sales, marketing focused to build awareness of your product or service, or online to build engagement with online customers and business networks.

Start writing here.

Marketing Strategy

Your strategy and marketing mix:

Guidance: Use this section to summarise the overall strategy and marketing mix (The 7 p's) you will use to position yourself within the market to meet your customers' needs. Your strategy and marketing mix should consider the activities that are relevant for your business. Remember to consider your digital strategy, which focuses on achieving your online objectives. Whatever your strategy, aim to differentiate yourself from your competitors to encourage customers to choose your business first.

Start writing here.

Action Steps

Top 10 Action Steps:

Guidance: Create a list of the Top 10 action steps that will bring your theoretical objectives (your marketing strategy and objectives) to life. E.g. Finish SWOT Activity Sheet, complete marketing budget}

Start writing here.

Background Analysis

The background analysis should give a snapshot of where you are right now, where you have been and where you want to go. Undertaking this process will help you to define your business's capabilities and find opportunities within your market. Finally, defining your core business elements will ensure that your marketing plan and overall business strategy work together seamlessly.

Start writing here.

Business overview

Guideline: The overview should cover the nuts and bolts of your business including:

The name, structure and date of establishment

Details about the owners (their names, roles and levels of experience etc.)

What your business is about (your business mission, vision and values)

The key business objectives you would like to achieve

An outline of the main products and services sold

A financial analysis of your business including sales and profitability

A SWOT analysis of your business to set a line in the sand

Business name:

Guidance: What's your business registered business name? If you haven't registered a business name, add your proposed business name here.

Start writing here.

Business structure:

Guidance: What's the formal structure of your business? Are you a sole trader, in a partnership, a trust or company?

22

ABN:

Guidance: What's your registered Australian Business Number?

ACN:

Guidance: What's your registered Australian Company Number, if applicable?

Business location:

Guidance: Where does your business operate from?

Date established:

Guidance: When did you begin trading?

Business owner(s):

Guidance: Who are the owners of the business?

Owner/s experience:

Guidance: Create a summary of your (and other owner's) experience in the industry and any major achievements/awards.

Vision statement:

Guidance: A Vision statement should describe WHERE you want your business to be in the future. It should communicate both the PURPOSE and VALUES of your business and answer the question, 'Why are we here?'

Mission statement:

Guidance: A Mission statement should outline HOW you will get to where you want your business to be in the future (Your Vision). It should define the PURPOSE and PRIMARY OBJECTIVES of your business and answer the question, 'What do we do?'

Business objectives:

Guidance: What are your short and long-term goals for your business?

Short Term goals:

Guidance: What are three primary short-term goals for your business (6 Months)?

Goal/Objective	Description	By when
{insert Goal/Objective name}	{insert Brief goal/objective description}	{insert Date of completion}

Long Term goals:

Guidance: What are three primary long-term goals for your business (1-3 Years)?

Goal/Objective	Description	By when
{insert Goal/Objective name}	{insert Brief goal/objective description}	{insert Date of completion}

Products:

Guidance: What products and/or services do you sell?

Product/Service	Description	Price
{insert Product/service name}	{insert Brief product/service description}	{insert Unit price including GST}

Financial Analysis

Guidance: In this section provide a high-level analysis of your current financial situation, specifically addressing sales and profitability.

Part 1 – Sales Analysis

Guidance: Use this section to summarise the current sales data for your industry (if available) and your business. The areas that you can analyse include:

- Sales for your overall market

- Sales for your business

- Sales for your competitors

If you wish to dig deeper, you can expand the analysis to Sales by Product Categories, Sales by Distribution Channels and Sales by Geography.

Start writing here.

Part 2 – Profitability Analysis

Guidance: Use the sales numbers above to identify realised revenues rather than just projections and then breakdown marketing expenses in terms of direct (expenses directly tied to products) and indirect or proportional (general administrative or broad marketing expenses).

Start writing here.

SWOT analysis

Guidance: Use the table below to list each of your businesses Strengths, Weaknesses, Opportunities or Threats (S.W.O.T.).

Strengths	Weaknesses
Start writing here	Start writing here
Opportunities	Threats
Start writing here	Start writing here

SWOT activity sheet

Guidance: Outline how and when you plan to address each of the weaknesses/threats from your SWOT analysis above.

SWOT weakness / threat	Activity to address weakness/threat	Completion date

The Market Overview

Guidance: Gathering information and identifying the key characteristics of your target market will help you to find the most effective way to reach your target customers. The Market Overview should provide an analysis of the market in which your business operates, including your customers, competitors and the market. Revisit this process regularly to ensure that your strategy remains relevant and targeted.

Start writing here.

Your Market

Target market:

Guidance: Summarise the key statistics for your target market. This may include the size and growth potential of your market, as well as key demographics such as age, gender, income level etc.

Start writing here.

Market research and environmental/industry analysis:

Guidance: What research have you completed to help analyse your market? Did you utilise a survey/questionnaire? If so, you may like to attach a copy of your survey/questionnaire and findings to the back of this plan. In this section, detail the results of the market research you have performed. Consider questions such as:

- Is the area experiencing population growth or decline?

- Does the region where you operate have a stable economy?

- Are there any seasonal variations that might affect sales?

- What is the size of the market?

- What recent trends have emerged in the market?

- Is there potential for growth in the market? How will you be able to capitalise on any opportunities?

- How will your entrance affect the market/customers?

- What external factors will affect your customers?

More information on DIY Market Research

Start writing here.

Your Customers

Target customers:

Guidance: Who are your target customers and how do they behave? Include specific demographics such as age, social status, education and gender. What are your customers' lifestyles, activities, values, needs, interests or opinions? Where are they located? Please adjust the column headings as required.

Customer	Age	Gender
{insert Target customer – choose a name}	{insert Customer's Age}	{insert Customer's Gender}
Ethnicity	**Education**	**Values**
{insert Customer's ethnic background}	{insert Customer's education level}	{insert Customer's values}

Customer profile:

Guidance: What's the profile of an ideal customer for your business? In a paragraph or two, clearly define your ideal customer - their needs, buying patterns and motivations for buying. This process will help you to develop a mental image of your ideal customer (often referred to as a customer avatar).

Your Competitors

Competitor analysis:

Guidance: Use the table below to analyse at least 5 competitors.}

Competitor	Established date	Size
{insert Competitor's name}	{insert When was their business established?}	{insert Number of staff and/or turnover}

Competitor profile:

Guidance: What's the profile of a typical competitor for your business? In a paragraph or two, clearly define a typical competitor - their size, market share, unique value proposition, strengths and weaknesses. This process will help you to develop a mental image of your typical competitor.

Start writing here.

Your Marketing

Marketing Objectives:

Guidance: Summarise the key marketing objectives for your business. Your objectives may be financial, with a goal to increase sales, or marketing focused, to build awareness of your product or service. An effective (and accountable) way to define your marketing objectives is to follow the 'SMART' acronym (Specific, Measurable, Achievable, Realistic and Timely)[1].

Examples of SMART marketing objectives

To achieve a 20% return on capital employed by April 2014 (Profitability Objective)

To gain 15% of the market for sports socks by November 2018 (Market Share Objective)

---

[1] Doran, G. T. (1981). There's a S.M.A.R.T. way to write management's goals and objectives. Management Review, Volume 70, Issue 11(AMA FORUM), pp. 35-36.

To make X brand of juice the preferred brand of 21-29-year-old females in Australia by August 2019 (Branding Objective)

Detail your SMART marketing objectives in the table below:

Objective	Specific	Measurable
{insert Your specific marketing objective}	{Is your objective specific?}	{Can your objective be measured?}
Achievable	**Realistic**	**Timely**
{Is your objective achievable?}	{Is your objective realistic?}	{Have you set a specific date for your objective to be achieved?}

Marketing Strategy

Guidance: Use this section to detail the overall strategy you will use to position yourself within the market to meet your customers' needs. Whatever your strategy, you goal should be to differentiate yourself from your competitors to encourage customers to choose your business first. The specific elements that make up your marketing strategy are typically referred to as the marketing mix. Each element can be varied to broaden the appeal of products and services and will therefore have a direct impact on sales.

The 8 P's of marketing

- Your PRODUCT (or SERVICE)

- The PRICING of your product or service

- Your POSITION (place) in the marketplace

- The PROMOTION of your product of service

- The PEOPLE in your business (salespeople, staff etc.)

- The PROCESS represents the buying experience

- The PHYSICAL environment where the good/services are presented

- PRODUCTIVITY and Quality is an essential part of meeting customer needs.

Your PRODUCT or service

Guidance: Here you should describe your long-term product strategy in detail. If you are providing a service, then you should consider your service(s) as your product(s).

You will need to consider:

- What features, and benefits do you offer?

- The unique selling position - what makes your product/service different from your competitors'?

- Potential spin-off products or services?

Product or Service	Features	Benefits
{What is your product or service?}	{What are the features of your product or service?	{What are the customer benefits of your product or service?}
Unique Selling Position	**Support**	**Spin Offs**
{What makes your product or service unique?}	{What additional support do you offer? E.g. Warranty, money back etc.}	{Are there any potential spin-off products or services you can offer?}

The PRICING of your product or service

Guidance: Price is a critical component of your marketing mix. Why? Because choosing the right price for your products or services will help you to maximise profits and build strong relationships with your customers. By pricing effectively, you will also avoid the serious financial consequences that can occur if you price too low (not enough profit) or too high (not enough sales).

Setting prices for your products and services might seem like a daunting task, however, it doesn't need to be. Just remember:

- You are in business to make a profit (and that's ok!)

- Most business owners under-price the value that they deliver

- Your sales and marketing strategy should defend your prices

Your overall pricing strategy will depend on your marketing, business and lifestyle objectives. So, before you start the research process spend some time defining your income (and net profit) aspirations. Also look at the small business expected income benchmarks on the ATO website.

Product or Service	Price	Costs
{What is your product or service?}	{What is the price of your product or service?}	{What is the total cost of selling your product or service?}
Net Profit	Comp. Price	Value
{What Net Profit is made from selling your product or service?}	{What is your competitor's pricing for this product or service?	{What unique value does your product or service offer/deliver?}

Your POSITION (Place) in the marketplace

Guidance: Place refers to the channels and locations for distributing your product, related information, and support services. This is how you will position your product or service in the marketplace.

This includes:

- The place where the product/service can be bought

- The distribution channels

Place represents the location where a product can be purchased. It is often referred to as the distribution channel. This may include any physical store (supermarket, departmental stores) as well as virtual stores (e-markets and e-malls) on the Internet. This is crucial as this provides the place utility to the consumer, which often becomes a deciding factor for the purchase of many products across multiple product categories.

Sales and distribution channels

Channel type	Products/ services	Percentage of sales (%)	Channel strategy
{e.g.} Shopfront, internet, direct mail, export or wholesale.	List all the products/ services sold via this channel	What percentage of overall sales do you expect to sell via this channel?	Why have you decided to use this channel type? How and when will you use it? What is the strategy behind using this channel type for this product/service?

The PROMOTION of your product or service

Guidance: State how you currently promote and market your business now (or intend to). Compare (where applicable) what your competitors do for promotion, noting what does and doesn't work for them as well as yourself. Regardless of how good your business is, if you don't promote it and tell people you exist, it's unlikely you will make many sales.

Promotion is more than selling and advertising your business. It's about attracting the right people to use and reuse your business. There are several techniques to use and they can be combined in various ways to create the most cost-effective strategy for your needs.

Detail your promotion techniques into six categories:

- Online

- Public relations

- Advertising

- Promotion

- Packaging or personal selling

- Branding

Direct marketing is often added to the marketing mix despite being part of advertising rather than marketing.

The PEOPLE in your business (salespeople, staff etc.)

Guidance: Every employee in your business (if you have them) can influence the marketing of your products and services. Knowledgeable and friendly staff can contribute to creating satisfied customers and can provide the unique selling experience that an organisation is often seeking.

If an outstanding team provides a competitive advantage, then the quality of recruitment and training becomes essential to achieving your marketing objectives.

Some questions to consider when assessing your team members:

- Are they prepared to talk with clients in detail about your products and services?

- Do you have training in place to drive constant improvement?

- Do your team understand the process for handling client interactions?

- Are staff members empowered to make decisions (and act) on the business's behalf?

- Do they have the communication skills to be effective?

- Do staff members 'live' your brand ?

Name	Job Title
{e.g. Mr Chris Brantley}	{e.g. Marketing/ Sales Manager}
Department	**Responsibilities**
{e.g. Sales}	{insert the main responsibilities of this position}

The PROCESS represents the buying experience

Guidance: Process represents the buying experience that the customer experiences when they buy your product or service. For example, the way that a fine bottle of wine is presented and served in a restaurant, the reaction of a business to a complaint or the speed of delivery in a fast food outlet.

A poor process, on the other hand, can undermine the other elements of the marketing mix. Budget airlines, for example, may offer very competitive headline prices, but if the final price is inflated by additional charges such as baggage charges and administrative fees, customers may begin to feel that they have been taken advantage of even if the final price is lower than other carriers.

Product or Service	The Process
{What is your product or service?}	{Outline the Process in point form}
Key Benefits	**Improvements**
{What are the key benefits for the customer?}	{What changes can you make to improve the process?}

PHYSICAL ENVIRONMENT where the good/services are presented

Guidance: The physical environment where your products or services are sold and delivered can have a significant impact upon how your customers experience your business. The physical environment represents the tangible aspects of selling your products and services, such as the quality of the furnishings in your consulting rooms or the design of your reception area. Creating a positive physical environment doesn't have to be costly – a vase full of fresh flowers can make a big difference.

Use the table below to outline the physical environments that your customers experience when they buy your products or services and any improvements you might be able to make.

Name	Selling Environment
{What is your product or service?}	{Where is the product or service sold?}
Delivery Environment	**Improvements**
{Where is the product or service delivered?}	{What changes can you make to improve the Physical Environment?}

PRODUCTIVITY is an essential part of meeting a customer's needs

Guidance: Improving productivity is an important factor in cost management; however, it also plays a key role in satisfying customer' needs. The more effective and efficient your marketing efforts are the more satisfied customers your business will create at a lower cost.

Here are some examples of strategies that could improve your marketing productivity:

- Improved Marketing Accounting – take time to understand where resources are being spent, customer value being created and where money is being made or lost.

- Marketing Alliances – share resources, ideas and opportunities with other organisations that service the same customers.

- Encourage Customer Involvement – increase customer satisfaction and lower costs by adding customers to the value chain e.g. Ask them to write guest posts for your blog.

Name	Job Title
{e.g. Mr Chris Brantley}	{e.g. Marketing/ Sales Manager}
Department	**Responsibilities**
{e.g. Sales}	{What are the main responsibilities of this position?}

Marketing Activity

Guidance: Once you have defined your marketing mix, the next step is to detail the specific activities that you will undertake to achieve your marketing objectives. As you create these activities, keep referring to your marketing mix – it will help you to assess which activities are worth the time and effort to implement.

What steps or activities will you undertake to achieve your marketing objectives?

Marketing activity/milestone	Person responsible	Date of expected completion
{Print advertising, online advertising, mail-out, giveaway, media release, event, website, blog/social media, public relations,	{Who is responsible for completing this task?}	{When do you expect to complete the marketing activity?}

branding and artwork, or publications and catalogues.}		
Cost ($)	**Success indicator**	
{Estimated cost of activity.}	{What indicator/ measureme nt result will need to be met before this activity is considered a success?}	

Your Finances

Marketing Budget {YEAR}

Guidance: To complete this marketing budget, you should rely heavily on your financial statements and projections. Double-click the table below to enter your details or attach your own budget at the back of this marketing plan.

Item	Jan
Marketing/promotion	
Marketing agency	
Radio advertising	
Television advertising	
Print advertising	
Online advertising	
Social media	
Web search optimisation	
Mailouts	
Giveaways	
Events	
Branding & artwork	
Merchandising	
Publications	
Catalogues	
More...	
Marketing/ promotion total	$0,00
Other	
Research	
Travel	
Postage	

Administration	
Incidentals	
More...	
Other total	$0,00
Total	$0,00

Organisational Implications

Guidance: Organisational implications are often overlooked when business owners tackle a marketing plan. For example, if your goal is to increase your customer base by 15% and therefore your staff by 10% - will you be able to house them in your current offices? Could you outsource some tasks? It's important to consider and document these decisions in your plan.

Outline any organisational implications, which you feel may affect the implementation of your marketing plan.

Start writing here.

Contingencies

Guidance: All plans in business should remain flexible (and adjustable) as you are often working with assumptions. The more planning you do, the better you will become at predicting. However, as you are learning the needs of your market - it is fair to say that some of your assumptions are going to fall short of expectation.

Use the space below to outline any contingencies (alternative options) which may assist if things don't go as planned.

Start writing here.

Monitoring/measurement Activities

Guidance: Reviewing the impact of your marketing should be a periodic activity. List the details of each review in the table below.

Marketing activity	Date of review
{Print advertising, online advertising, mail-outs, giveaways, media releases, events, website, blog/social media, public relations, branding and artwork, or publications and catalogues.}	{e.g. Month/Year}
Monitoring methods	**Review outcomes**
{What tools did you use to measure/monitor the impact of your marketing activities?}	{e.g. What were the results for the promotional period? What were your sales/profit figures? How many new/repeat customers did you receive? How many customers visited your website? Etc.}

Supporting Documentation

Guidance: Attach any supporting documentation in relation to this marketing plan.

List all your attachments here. These may include resumes, customer survey/questionnaire and/or financial documents.

Start writing here.

Glossary

Term	Definition
Australian Business Number (ABN)	A unique identifying number used when dealing with other businesses and the Australian Tax Office.
Australian Company Number (ACN)	The number allocated by the Australian Securities and Investments Commission (ASIC) when you register a company under the Corporations Law.
Blog	A shortened word for Weblog (see Weblog).
Channel	A way of delivering something to its destination, whether it is a message to be communicated or a physical product to be delivered.
Contract	A legally enforceable agreement made between two or more parties. A contract may be a verbal contract or a written contract (or may be partly verbal and partly written).
Demographics	The characteristics of a population or segment of the population, commonly examined demographics include age, gender, ethnicity, knowledge of languages, employment status, mobility and geographic location.

Term	Definition
Domain name	An identification string (name) that identifies an organisation's address on the internet, either a website address or an email address. Domain names are formed by the rules and procedures of the Domain Name System (DNS). Read more information about Domain Name System on Wikipedia.
Blog	(also known as a weblog) an individual's or organisation's online website displaying a reverse-chronological list of entries (known as posts). Posts typically include thoughts, observations, promotions, links, images or videos. A Weblog is publicly available and allows readers to comment on posts.
Goods and Services Tax (GST)	A broad-based tax of 10 per cent on the sale of most goods and services in Australia.
High-end	Usually refers to expensive or high-quality products/services.
Market position	Refers to the position an organisation, product or service has in the market, usually in relation to its competition.

Term	Definition
Milestone	A goal or objective with a target date.
Mission statement	A statement (usually internally facing) which outlines how a business (organisation) intends to achieve its Vision. It should define the PURPOSE and PRIMARY OBJECTIVES of the business and answer the question, 'What do we do?'
Social media	A group of technology including Blogs, online networks (e.g. Twitter, Facebook, Myspace, LinkedIn) and online collaboration tools often used to expand your network/market reach or collaborate on a large scale.
Unique selling position	A characteristic of a business or a product/service that sets it apart from the competition.
Vision statement	A statement (usually public facing) which outlines where a business (organisation) wants to be in the future. It should communicate both the PURPOSE and VALUES of the business and answer the question, 'Why are we here?'

Acknowledgements and Reference

This template has been written in line with the guide provided by Business dot Vic company, and several business textbooks.

www.ingramcontent.com/pod-product-compliance
Lightning Source LLC
Chambersburg PA
CBHW021927170526
45157CB00005B/2215